always

always

TEAYUH

Copyright © 2021 by teayuh
All rights reserved, including the right to reproduce, distribute, or transmit in any form or by any means.

Edited by teayuh
Cover design by teayuh

ISBN 979-8-73605-759-7

Manufactured in the United States of America

First Edition July 2021

Dedicated to the loved and broken.

One day, you will be okay.
So please, keep pushing forward for that day.

always *teayuh*

you make me feel
even if you're not meaning to

you made me realize I had never been in love
before you
you showed me what it means to forgive,
even if they do not deserve forgiveness
and that just because there is pain to an ending
does not mean that pain is endless

I once told you that you make me want to be better,
and even after everything we've gone through,
separately or together,
messy or uplifting,
difficult or relieving,
it's still true

you make me feel
even if you're not meaning to

always   teayuh

I find that forgiving myself
is much more difficult
than asking others for forgiveness

always   teayuh

some have said I am wasting my time
and some say I deserve better

it is not my job to convince anyone
that what I feel is true
my truth is mine alone

and this is a reminder to all
that even the truth can be altered,
no matter how you may fight to maintain it

the hardest part is an understatement
one can never truly describe

I'm sorry it all meant so little to you
when it was everything to me

always *teayuh*

perhaps,
looking back,
I could've said the wrong thing

I could've shared the wrong story or song

I could've fought harder,
spoke softer,
maybe held my head higher

yet I will always believe
everything happens for a reason

perhaps,
looking back,
I wouldn't have changed any of it

always   *teayuh*

I think the reason we try to avoid heartbreak
at all costs
is because pain has been perceived as a destroyer
since the beginning

I believe the purpose of pain is not to run from it
but to allow yourself to feel it
allow yourself to learn the lesson
in which it is attached to
and grow from it

what if pain is not a destroyer

what if pain is a guide

always   teayuh

looking back,
there was darkness

looking forward,
there's you

my light

always *teayuh*

and though I have sleepless nights...
I'll wake and my eyes are swollen from the tears

I'll bend over,
trying to salvage my joy,
but that ache in my chest causes me to stumble

and though I miss the conversations...
the little things
the miniscule moments

and though I could have saved myself
from the trenches

the love I have felt and continue to feel,
indescribable and unforgettable,
I wouldn't give it up for anything

always　　　　　*teayuh*

I want to be held by you
I want to take in your scent
and feel your arms embrace me
I want to touch your skin

whisper sweet nothings in my ear
caress my cheek and let me look into your eyes

I want to see you
I want you to see me

to be held by you is my heaven on earth

always   *teayuh*

until the end of this life,
far into the next,
beyond the soul and the fear it holds,
the capacity in which I love will expand

I knew not the power of emotion
until you glanced my way
and I was gone

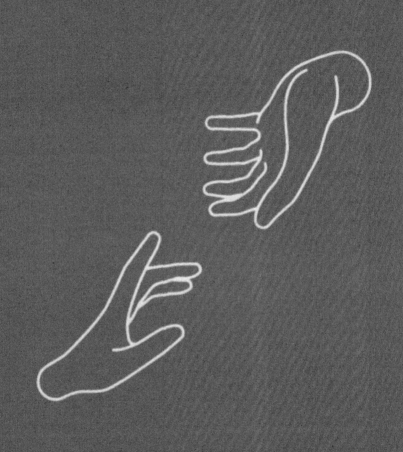

always *teayuh*

to give and to get

the action of giving is not love
the action of receiving is not love

the thought of a person
thinking of someone is to love
the giving

the appreciation of a person
being thankful of someone is to love
the getting

to give and to get

always   *teayuh*

they can do what they want with me

they can drag my spirit through broken glass
they can spew hatred from their tongues

they can even pick me apart,
piece by piece,
until my character is viewed as nothing more than flawed

but they cannot touch him

I will not allow anyone to disturb my peace

always   *teayuh*

                                                         should I be less?
                                                   if I became less,
                          would it be enough for you?

I would lay down my everything in an instant
                 if it meant I could spend time with you

                                     I sacrifice my happiness
                                         I sacrifice my hurt

                                           should I be less?
                                         if I become less,
                              will it be enough for you?

always   *teayuh*

I know that you didn't mean everything you said to me

you didn't lie
you just didn't know you weren't telling me the truth

I feel I don't have the right to be upset
because you weren't aware
and that is what hurts the most

always *teayuh*

even if it wasn't 'meant to be'
how thankful I am
that it 'was'

always *teayuh*

I have to learn to be okay without you

I have to find company in myself
I have to trust myself
I have to give myself the love I want to give to others

I have to be okay without you
so I can possibly be great with you
someday

always   *teayuh*

understand that the acceptance
is the most trying

it is my love for you
that keeps me afloat

I am here,
pining quietly,
supporting violently,
yet still hanging onto hope

always   *teayuh*

I didn't want your all
I didn't want your perfection
I never wanted the side you show to others
when you practice retroflection

what I want doesn't matter
and what you share is your choice to make
a friend to you until the end
beside you now
and far past your wake

because even if I'm not
your favorite person anymore
you are still mine
and I can always find comfort in knowing
I was yours
once upon a time

always   teayuh

                                                I will laugh
and I will smile
I will continue waking up to the sun
when I know all the while
you'll be with her
and she'll be shining
and I hope your late-night thoughts become a memory
and you forget about all the crying

I hope you both are able to pick up the pieces
and create a new work of art
I hope she never takes you for granted
again and tears your soul apart

because I saw your stitching
and I had tried to guide your hand
and you let me help for a moment or two
until you retreated back
but I still understand

⟶

always *teayuh*

I wish you happiness
and I wish you love
not just for each other but for yourself
and I hope this new beginning for you
will provide you with emotional wealth

so I will laugh
and I will smile
I will continue waking up to the sun
when I know all the while
you'll be with her
and she'll be shining
and I hope your late-night thoughts become a memory
and you forget about all the crying

always   teayuh

I knew something had changed
when I told you I was listening to music
and you no longer asked
'What song?'

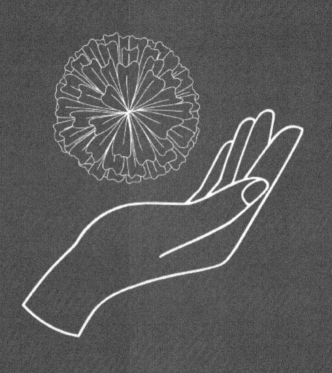

always *teayuh*

I hope you know

I hope you know that I could never blame you
for the way that I feel

I hope you know I hold no hatred in my heart,
only hurt

I hope you know how special you are to me,
even on the days we barely talk

I hope you know how much you've impacted my life
in the little time we've shared

I hope you know how much I want for you
how much I care for you
how much I hope for you

I hope you know
that you'll never know
how much I love you

always   *teayuh*

~~do you think of me as often as I think of you?~~

~~I miss you and I look forward to hearing from you,~~
~~even if it's no longer every day~~

~~I want you to know that I knew I was going to get hurt~~
~~but I didn't care~~

~~you're worth it and have always been worth it~~

hey,
how have you been?

always *teayuh*

I've bitten my lip raw
there's no more tears to shed
heart rate slower now
trying to put thoughts of you to bed

always   *teayuh*

the fact that you exist
turns your stomach
and clouds your vision

you won't touch a child
for the fear that a part of you will stay with them
and how could you ever forgive yourself
for tainting such innocence?

how could you ever forgive yourself
for carrying the lies of the dishonest
while trying to find worth in your truth?

forgive your fears,
your blurred vision,
and the weight that you hold

I have never seen such beauty
in the eyes that hold the most pain

always   teayuh

I feel blessed
you even took a chance on me
in the first place

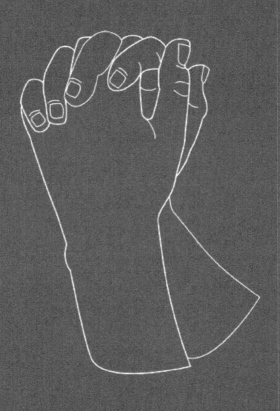

always   teayuh

we were driving late one night
conversing about the ways of the world
I was in the passenger seat
and you were driving my car

I remember you turning to me
you grabbed my hand and said,
"As long as you're by my side,
I know I can get through anything."

the ways of the world may have caught up
but I'm still here

always   *teayuh*

when did I know?

~~when you asked me to rub your back for the first time~~

~~when you would randomly grab my hand and spin me around~~

~~when you were comfortable enough to ask me to shower with you~~

~~when you were patient enough to teach me to be comfortable with cuddling~~

~~when you defended me from your own flesh and blood~~

I knew the first time you asked me
to go on an adventure
that there was no going back

always   teayuh

there are no gifts to be given
words to be said
or thoughts to be acted upon
that could ever measure up
to how thankful I am
to have you in my life

maybe it was fate

maybe it was destiny

maybe it was something foretold in a dream

maybe

just maybe

things are not as they seem

always   *teayuh*

                       I can't say that I'm the only one
                       you've shared your secrets with

                       I can't say that I'm the only one
                                 you confide in

                       I can't say that I'm the only one
                                     you trust

                       and I would never want to

                       how selfish that would be
               to have your everything to myself
knowing that I am not everything that you need

always   *teayuh*

I am so proud of you
for challenging the limits you set for yourself
and setting the boundaries
you never thought you could

as you step into this new chapter
I will continue to be proud
even if I never get to see the next one

always   *teayuh*

of course I don't want to lose you

I want you in my life
forever

losing you is my biggest fear

always   *teayuh*

you're my person
but I'll never be yours

maybe in another life

everything is different now
you are never going to care like you once did
and I am always going to care too much

this guessing game
I so desperately want to quit playing

can I be straightforward with you?
are we going to go on forever as strangers
pretending we've stayed great friends?

to say we deserve better
when we can work on being better
words no longer hold meaning
they are just a cop out

always   *teayuh*

I never know anymore

I ask you if you want me to be in your life
when I should be asking
if you want to be in mine

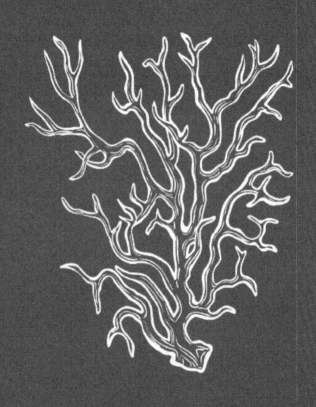

always *teayuh*

do not assume my feelings for you
do not believe your assumptions to be fact
do not come to me
highlighting what I didn't say or show
if you ignored what I did

I'm talking to myself too

always   *teayuh*

I will never let them
be right about you
because everything they say you are...
I know you're not

always *teayuh*

saying you were shutting me out
was a poor choice of words
you were just pushing me away

maybe it was low energy
maybe you were changing
or maybe,
just maybe,
you thought you were protecting me

someone you let too close
but didn't realize it
until you felt it was too late

how confusing it must be
knowing that,
despite your best efforts,
I have never budged

always *teayuh*

the sun will greet me
in all her warmth
but the memory of your arms around me
only makes her feel cold

the moon will try to catch my attention
he glows fiercely in the darkness
but the memory of your half-smile
only makes him a blur

from day to night
and night to day
you are my first thought when I awake
and my last thought before I drift

and so
the cycle continues

always   teayuh

                    you believed me to be in your life
                                    to help you
                in the way you thought you needed

                                        only,
                  I know it is much more than that
              I have had to learn what you have lived

                                to love someone
                    who does not love you in return

always   *teayuh*

because I care

...

that's it

always   teayuh

a mind worth keeping
is a mind that is committed
to take all on
when all seems impossible

always   teayuh

hesitation
doubt
guessing

they'll never exist when it comes to you

always   *teayuh*

it amazes me how one person can come into your life and leave in such a hurry by the next day.
the next day follows with absolute agony, an absolute gut wrenching loss... then they return with a bandage to win a temporary smile and act as if nothing happened.
you build that wall, again and again, that they made the blueprints for... reusing the same bandage for an infected wound.

always   *teayuh*

for what it's worth
I knew this day would come
and for what it's worth
I'll be okay

always   teayuh

because an act of love takes two
and an act of disrespect takes one

always   *teayuh*

you are my best ~~friend~~
                 decision

always *teayuh*

I apologize for taking things too personally
even if you are unaware of the war inside my head

I've just never cared so much for another before
and I'm still learning how to handle it

always   *teayuh*

can only hope
I've done enough right by you
to be remembered
when I'm gone

always   teayuh

infinitely intertwined
despite illness

I see you

always   *teayuh*

when you look at me
it's like a splash of water colors

sunlight reflecting off of stained glass

leaves changing during autumn

the northern lights

it's everything that is beautiful
all at once

always   *teayuh*

may peace be with you while you are your only company
and may peace be with you
when
and if
you decide to reach out again

always   teayuh

I find it astonishing that,
despite us having different backgrounds,
different stories,
different books,
different chapters,

we've landed on the same page

always   *teayuh*

all I wish for myself
is that I can someday be loved
as much as,
and in the way that,
I love you

and for you,
I hope,
when you are ready,
you are able to accept a love like that

an 'always' kind of love
comes once in a lifetime

always

TEAYUH

| Meet The Author |

teayuh is a small town native of western Massachusetts. She found a love for poetry at seven years old and has been writing ever since, whether it be to pass the time or to share with the world.

teayuh has always found it easier to express her thoughts and feelings through writing and considers writing her safe place. She always hopes that her work helps others to realize that they are not alone in their emotions.

"I can listen no longer in silence. I must speak to you by such means as are within my reach. You pierce my soul. I am half agony, half hope."

~ Jane Austen

Made in the USA
Middletown, DE
28 July 2024